KU-789-142

Ginn Mathematics 5

REINFORCEMENT TEXTBOOK

GINN

Adding

Step 1.
Add units.

```
  35
+ 23
─────
   8
```

Step 2.
Add tens.

```
  35
+ 23
─────
  58
```

Copy and complete.

1	53 +14	2	47 +31	3	35 +20	4	72 +26	5	38 +40
6	84 +31	7	66 +22	8	37 +52	9	86 +40	10	92 +37
11	43 +43	12	20 +39	13	38 +21	14	42 +56	15	56 +42
16	221 +314	17	506 +213	18	425 +212	19	604 +352	20	672 +325
21	251 +346	22	763 +406	23	152 +347	24	370 +426	25	438 +940

More adding

Step 1.	Step 2.	Step 3.
Add units, regroup.	Add tens.	Add hundreds.

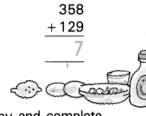

Step 1.
```
  358
+ 129
-----
    7
```

Step 2.
```
  358
+ 129
-----
   87
```

Step 3.
```
  358
+ 129
-----
  487
```

Copy and complete.

1
```
  27
+ 35
----
```

2
```
  36
+ 49
----
```

3
```
  42
+ 28
----
```

4
```
  75
+ 18
----
```

5
```
  23
+ 59
----
```

6
```
  45
+ 37
----
```

7
```
  68
+ 27
----
```

8
```
  54
+ 39
----
```

9
```
  67
+ 26
----
```

10
```
  75
+ 18
----
```

11
```
  375
+ 218
-----
```

12
```
  427
+ 365
-----
```

13
```
  269
+ 205
-----
```

14
```
  726
+ 259
-----
```

15
```
  483
+ 409
-----
```

16
```
  583
+ 275
-----
```

17
```
  542
+ 376
-----
```

18
```
  570
+ 353
-----
```

19
```
  591
+ 265
-----
```

20
```
  364
+ 245
-----
```

21
```
  237
+ 491
-----
```

22
```
  729
+ 190
-----
```

23
```
  632
+ 287
-----
```

24
```
  251
+ 384
-----
```

25
```
  375
+ 252
-----
```

An addition riddle

Add these. Then decode the riddle.

1	2	3	4	5
49 +43	63 +64	126 +49	208 +88	56 +37
___ A	___ B	___ C	___ D	___ E

6	7	8	9	10
166 +218	172 +146	232 +439	573 +271	271 +335
___ F	___ G	___ H	___ I	___ J

11	12	13	14	15
392 +476	450 +392	234 +216	37 +28	147 +381
___ K	___ L	___ M	___ N	___ O

16	17	18	19	20
405 +507	83 +31	160 +453	746 +90	25 +38
___ P	___ R	___ S	___ T	___ U

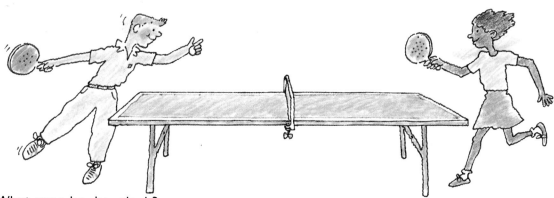

What goes ha, ha, clonk?
92   450 92 65   842 92 63 318 671 844 65 318   671 844 613

671 93 92 296   528 384 384

Estimating and adding

I can estimate the sum.

Estimate the sum and write down the correct letter.
Do **not** add the numbers yet.

1	59 +23	(a) 62 (b) 72 (c) 82 (d) 92	2	21 +49	(a) 50 (b) 60 (c) 70 (d) 80	3	38 +19	(a) 67 (b) 47 (c) 57 (d) 77
4	78 +63	(a) 131 (b) 141 (c) 151 (d) 161	5	69 +88	(a) 157 (b) 137 (c) 167 (d) 147	6	91 +73	(a) 144 (b) 154 (c) 174 (d) 164
7	618 +289	(a) 807 (b) 707 (c) 907 (d) 1007	8	423 +315	(a) 738 (b) 1038 (c) 938 (d) 638	9	729 +472	(a) 1101 (b) 1301 (c) 1001 (d) 1201
10	536 +782	(a) 1358 (b) 1318 (c) 1398 (d) 1388	11	923 +218	(a) 1101 (b) 1111 (c) 1141 (d) 1181	12	658 +497	(a) 1155 (b) 1135 (c) 1165 (d) 1175
13	765 +346	(a) 1101 (b) 1001 (c) 1111 (d) 1141	14	985 +370	(a) 1255 (b) 1295 (c) 1305 (d) 1355	15	601 +583	(a) 1284 (b) 1184 (c) 1154 (d) 1194

Go back and add to find each sum.
How many did you get right by estimating?

More addition

Step 1.
Add units
and regroup.

```
  236
+ 829
─────
    5
```

Step 2.
Add tens.

```
  236
+ 829
─────
   65
```

Step 3.
Add hundreds

```
  236
+ 829
─────
 1065
```

Copy and complete.

1
```
  892
+ 654
─────
```

2
```
  934
+ 869
─────
```

3
```
  356
+ 955
─────
```

4
```
  439
+ 865
─────
```

5
```
  974
+ 974
─────
```

6
```
  275
+ 848
─────
```

7
```
  584
+ 637
─────
```

8
```
  696
+ 508
─────
```

9
```
  837
+ 693
─────
```

10
```
  239
+ 982
─────
```

11
```
  564
+ 489
─────
```

12
```
  438
+ 869
─────
```

13
```
   46
   29
+  18
─────
```

14
```
   63
    8
+  27
─────
```

15
```
   84
   13
+  36
─────
```

16
```
   39
   23
   18
+  14
─────
```

17
```
   44
   35
   38
+   9
─────
```

18
```
  215
  316
+ 278
─────
```

19
```
  467
   96
+ 384
─────
```

20
```
  597
  148
+ 366
─────
```

21
```
  134
  287
   86
+ 467
─────
```

22
```
  555
  328
  196
+ 686
─────
```

Adding money

How much money?

Add these:

6   14p
     + 28p
	7 45p
	     + 29p
		8 74p
		     + 6p
			9 84p
			     + 27p

10   £1.46
    + £3.16
	11 £0.84
	    + £2.29
		12 £4.83
		    + £2.97
			13 £5.56
			    + 68p

14   £3.87
    + 95p
	15 77p
	    + £1.48
		16 £6.87
		    + £8.96
			17 £9.42
			    + £9.99

Solve

18 Tracy had £3.49 and Gran gave her £6.84 for shopping.
How much did Tracy have altogether?

19 Eddie had £4.18 and Sarah had £2.88.
How much did they have altogether?

Cross-number puzzle. Addition and subtraction

Copy the cross-number square.

First solve all the **across** clues. Then solve any **down** clues that you need to complete the puzzle.

Check your work by solving the rest of the **down** clues.

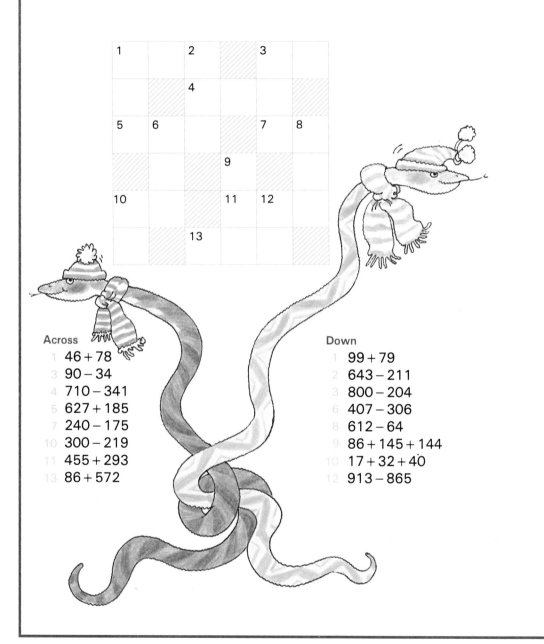

Across

1. 46 + 78
3. 90 − 34
4. 710 − 341
5. 627 + 185
7. 240 − 175
10. 300 − 219
11. 455 + 293
13. 86 + 572

Down

1. 99 + 79
2. 643 − 211
3. 800 − 204
6. 407 − 306
8. 612 − 64
9. 86 + 145 + 144
10. 17 + 32 + 40
12. 913 − 865

Subtraction

Step 1.
There are not enough units so regroup 1 ten for 10 units.

$$\begin{array}{r} 6\overset{6}{7}\overset{1}{4} \\ -435 \\ \hline \end{array}$$

Step 2.
Subtract units.

$$\begin{array}{r} 6\overset{6}{7}\overset{1}{4} \\ -435 \\ \hline 9 \end{array}$$

Step 3.
Subtract tens.

$$\begin{array}{r} 6\overset{6}{7}\overset{1}{4} \\ -435 \\ \hline 39 \end{array}$$

Step 4.
Subtract hundreds.

$$\begin{array}{r} 6\overset{6}{7}\overset{1}{4} \\ -435 \\ \hline 239 \end{array}$$

Copy and complete.

1. $\begin{array}{r} 87 \\ -23 \\ \hline \end{array}$ 2. $\begin{array}{r} 65 \\ -14 \\ \hline \end{array}$ 3. $\begin{array}{r} 78 \\ -35 \\ \hline \end{array}$ 4. $\begin{array}{r} 94 \\ -42 \\ \hline \end{array}$ 5. $\begin{array}{r} 62 \\ -50 \\ \hline \end{array}$

6. $\begin{array}{r} 58 \\ -32 \\ \hline \end{array}$ 7. $\begin{array}{r} 97 \\ -16 \\ \hline \end{array}$ 8. $\begin{array}{r} 81 \\ -20 \\ \hline \end{array}$ 9. $\begin{array}{r} 59 \\ -42 \\ \hline \end{array}$ 10. $\begin{array}{r} 46 \\ -35 \\ \hline \end{array}$

11. $\begin{array}{r} 571 \\ -138 \\ \hline \end{array}$ 12. $\begin{array}{r} 756 \\ -218 \\ \hline \end{array}$ 13. $\begin{array}{r} 677 \\ -339 \\ \hline \end{array}$ 14. $\begin{array}{r} 727 \\ -361 \\ \hline \end{array}$ 15. $\begin{array}{r} 948 \\ -195 \\ \hline \end{array}$

16. $\begin{array}{r} 425 \\ -284 \\ \hline \end{array}$ 17. $\begin{array}{r} 817 \\ -562 \\ \hline \end{array}$ 18. $\begin{array}{r} 509 \\ -373 \\ \hline \end{array}$

19. $\begin{array}{r} 954 \\ -162 \\ \hline \end{array}$ 20. $\begin{array}{r} 622 \\ -491 \\ \hline \end{array}$ 21. $\begin{array}{r} 493 \\ -288 \\ \hline \end{array}$

22. $\begin{array}{r} 563 \\ -271 \\ \hline \end{array}$ 23. $\begin{array}{r} 380 \\ -238 \\ \hline \end{array}$ 24. $\begin{array}{r} 362 \\ -290 \\ \hline \end{array}$

Estimating and subtracting

$$\begin{array}{r} 302 \\ -178 \\ \hline \end{array}$$

Round to the nearest 10 ⟩ $$\begin{array}{r} 300 \\ -180 \\ \hline 120 \end{array}$$

Round to the nearest 10 ⟩

$$\begin{array}{r} {\scriptstyle 2\ \overset{9}{\cancel{\scriptstyle\cancel{0}}}\ {}_1} \\ 302 \\ -178 \\ \hline 124 \end{array}$$

The answer (124) is close to the estimate (120).

First round each number to the nearest 10 and estimate the difference.
Then subtract and check that your answer is close to your estimate.

1. $$\begin{array}{r} 965 \\ -398 \\ \hline \end{array}$$

2. $$\begin{array}{r} 734 \\ -557 \\ \hline \end{array}$$

3. $$\begin{array}{r} 862 \\ -299 \\ \hline \end{array}$$

4. $$\begin{array}{r} 316 \\ -258 \\ \hline \end{array}$$

5. $$\begin{array}{r} 531 \\ -172 \\ \hline \end{array}$$

6. $$\begin{array}{r} 826 \\ -259 \\ \hline \end{array}$$

7. $$\begin{array}{r} 625 \\ -378 \\ \hline \end{array}$$

8. $$\begin{array}{r} 915 \\ -459 \\ \hline \end{array}$$

9. $$\begin{array}{r} 827 \\ -459 \\ \hline \end{array}$$

10. $$\begin{array}{r} 736 \\ -498 \\ \hline \end{array}$$

11. $$\begin{array}{r} 647 \\ -358 \\ \hline \end{array}$$

12. $$\begin{array}{r} 958 \\ -179 \\ \hline \end{array}$$

13. $$\begin{array}{r} 226 \\ -157 \\ \hline \end{array}$$

14. $$\begin{array}{r} 713 \\ -486 \\ \hline \end{array}$$

15. $$\begin{array}{r} 444 \\ -285 \\ \hline \end{array}$$

16. $$\begin{array}{r} 768 \\ -399 \\ \hline \end{array}$$

17. $$\begin{array}{r} 973 \\ -774 \\ \hline \end{array}$$

18. $$\begin{array}{r} 624 \\ -387 \\ \hline \end{array}$$

19. $$\begin{array}{r} 638 \\ -349 \\ \hline \end{array}$$

20. $$\begin{array}{r} 457 \\ -298 \\ \hline \end{array}$$

21. $$\begin{array}{r} 602 \\ -148 \\ \hline \end{array}$$

22. $$\begin{array}{r} 513 \\ -247 \\ \hline \end{array}$$

23. $$\begin{array}{r} 602 \\ -313 \\ \hline \end{array}$$

24. $$\begin{array}{r} 900 \\ -458 \\ \hline \end{array}$$

Brackets

Copy and complete.

watch the signs!

1 (376 + 521) − 536 = ___

3 (814 + 131) − 827 = ___

5 (743 − 179) − 531 = ___

7 (486 + 451) − 119 = ___

9 (554 − 330) + 387 = ___

11 (143 + 258) − 299 = ___

13 792 − (107 + 429) = ___

15 561 − (301 − 142) = ___

17 179 + (360 + 179) = ___

19 704 + (573 − 268) = ___

2 (419 − 289) + 487 = ___

4 (992 − 350) − 439 = ___

6 (217 + 307) − 405 = ___

8 (275 + 394) + 495 = ___

10 (622 + 178) − 456 = ___

12 (243 + 456) + 532 = ___

14 232 + (69 + 499) = ___

16 423 + (671 + 617) = ___

18 347 − (961 − 879) = ___

20 919 − (432 + 486) = ___

Plane shapes

Make a list of things in the picture which are very nearly
(a) squares (b) rectangles (c) triangles (d) circles.

For instance, the television screen is nearly a rectangle (the corners are rounded).

Solids

A

B

C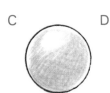

D

E

F

Give the letter by the solid that is:

1 a cube

2 a cuboid

3 a sphere

4 a cylinder

5 a cone

6 a pyramid

Who am I?
Name the solid.

7

I have
no vertices.

8

I have only
1 flat surface.

9 I have 6 flat surfaces
that are squares.

10 I have 8 vertices and my edges
are not all the same length.

11 I have 5 flat surfaces.

12 I have no flat surfaces.

13 I have 8 edges
and 5 vertices.

14 I have only 2 flat surfaces.

15 I have 12 edges
all the same length.

16 I have 3 surfaces
and 1 is curved.

The 24-hour clock

We use the 24-hour clock for air and railway timetables. There is no need to use a.m. or p.m. with the 24-hour clock.

For example:

5:00 a.m.

24-hour clock time 05:00

5:00 p.m.

17:00

Here are some other examples:

8:30 a.m.

08:30

4:15 p.m.

16:15

11:48 p.m.

23:48

12:09 a.m.

00.09

Give the 24-hour clock time.

1 5:20 a.m.	2 6:00 a.m.	3 9:57 a.m.	4 10:30 a.m.
5 11:45 a.m.	6 12:00 noon	7 1:00 p.m.	8 2:00 p.m.
9 4:00 p.m.	10 6:25 p.m.	11 8:45 p.m.	12 10:40 p.m.

Write each time using a.m. or p.m.

13 01:00	14 04:30	15 09:50	16 11:40
17 12:45	18 13:30	19 15:45	20 16:05
21 19:00	22 21:30	23 22:45	24 23:15

Timetable problems

The bus leaves Bugton at 10:27 and arrives at Wormham 18 minutes later. It waits 5 minutes at Wormham and then takes 24 minutes to reach Spiderville. It leaves Spiderville at 11:33 and travels to Beetlehurst, arriving at 12:04.

1 At what time does the bus (a) arrive at Wormham?
   (b) leave Wormham?
   (c) arrive at Spiderville?

2 How long did it take to go from Spiderville to Beetlehurst?

3 (a) What was the total time taken for the journey from Bugton to Beetlehurst?
   (b) How long altogether was the bus waiting at the bus stops?
   (c) How long altogether was the bus moving?

4 Another bus left Bugton at 11:04 and arrived in Beetlehurst at quarter past 1.
   (a) Which bus took longer, the 10:27 bus or the 11:04 bus?
   (b) How much longer did it take?

5 Write the times of any bus or train journey you go on. (Make them up if you like!) Make up some questions like the ones above. Give them to your friends to answer. Then you can answer your friends' questions.

A riddle

Find the change. Then decode to find a message.

	You have	You spend	Change				You have	You spend	Change	
1	£5	£2.98	—	A		2	£10	£6.05	—	D
3	£1	£0.86	—	E		4	£20	£9.83	—	G
5	£2	£1.74	—	I		6	£5	£4.31	—	N
7	£10	£0.97	—	O		8	£1	£0.06	—	P
9	£20	£12.39	—	S		10	£0.75	£0.57	—	T
11	£5	£4.92	—	V		12	£10	£9.26	—	Y

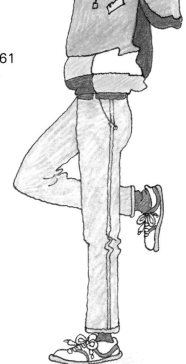

£2.02   £0.94 £0.14 £0.69 £0.69 £0.74

£7.61 £2.02 £0.08 £0.14 £3.95   £0.26 £7.61

£2.02   £0.94 £0.14 £0.69 £0.69 £0.74

£10.17 £2.02 £0.26 £0.69 £0.14 £3.95

Money problems

Find the total cost of these snacks.

1 Cheese sandwich
   Bar of chocolate
   Glass of milk

2 Apple
   Packet of crisps
   Bar of chocolate

3 Packet of crisps
   Glass of milk
   Apple

4 Cheese sandwich
   Apple
   Glass of milk
   Packet of crisps

5 Apple
   Glass of milk
   Packet of crisps
   Bar of chocolate

6 Cheese sandwich
   Apple
   Glass of milk
   Bar of chocolate

7 Alan bought a cheese sandwich and a glass of milk.
   He paid with a £5 note. How much change did he receive?

8 Tariq bought an apple, a glass of milk and a cheese sandwich.
   (a) What was the total cost?
   (b) How much money did he have left out of £4.08?

9 Claire has a glass of milk, an apple and a bar of chocolate every school day.
   (a) How much does she spend each day?
   (b) What is the total cost in a school week?

Multiplication and addition

Complete each multiplication-addition puzzle.

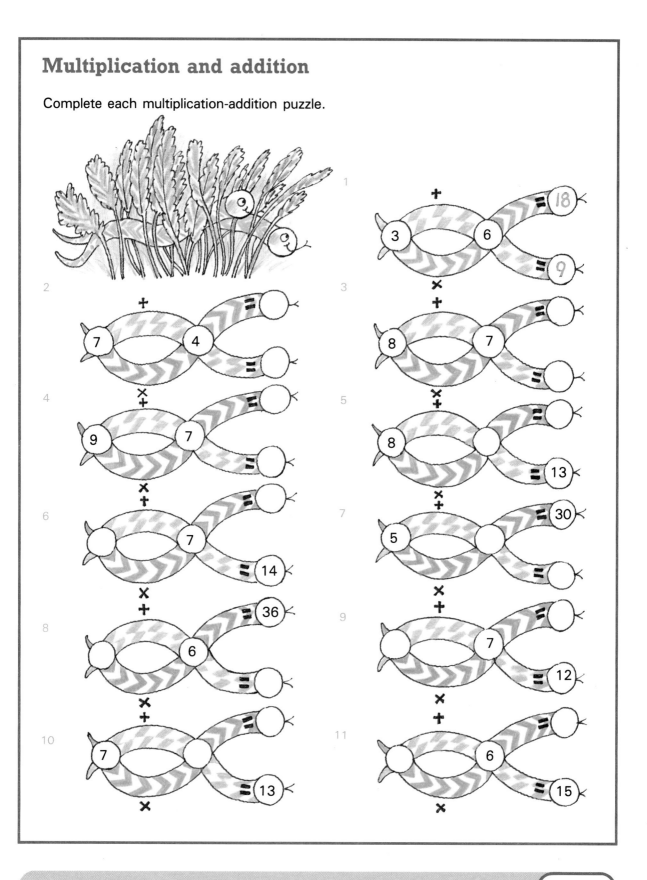

Multiplication

Copy and complete.

1 $\begin{array}{r}8\\ \times 2\\ \hline 16\end{array}$	2 $\begin{array}{r}3\\ \times 4\\ \hline \end{array}$	3 $\begin{array}{r}6\\ \times 7\\ \hline \end{array}$	4 $\begin{array}{r}5\\ \times 3\\ \hline \end{array}$	5 $\begin{array}{r}7\\ \times 5\\ \hline \end{array}$	6 $\begin{array}{r}6\\ \times 3\\ \hline \end{array}$
7 $\begin{array}{r}6\\ \times 2\\ \hline \end{array}$	8 $\begin{array}{r}3\\ \times 9\\ \hline \end{array}$	9 $\begin{array}{r}2\\ \times 7\\ \hline \end{array}$	10 $\begin{array}{r}6\\ \times 4\\ \hline \end{array}$	11 $\begin{array}{r}6\\ \times 8\\ \hline \end{array}$	12 $\begin{array}{r}7\\ \times 4\\ \hline \end{array}$
13 $\begin{array}{r}9\\ \times 6\\ \hline \end{array}$	14 $\begin{array}{r}8\\ \times 3\\ \hline \end{array}$	15 $\begin{array}{r}9\\ \times 4\\ \hline \end{array}$	16 $\begin{array}{r}7\\ \times 2\\ \hline \end{array}$	17 $\begin{array}{r}8\\ \times 7\\ \hline \end{array}$	18 $\begin{array}{r}5\\ \times 9\\ \hline \end{array}$
19 $\begin{array}{r}6\\ \times 5\\ \hline \end{array}$	20 $\begin{array}{r}7\\ \times 8\\ \hline \end{array}$	21 $\begin{array}{r}5\\ \times 4\\ \hline \end{array}$	22 $\begin{array}{r}7\\ \times 7\\ \hline \end{array}$	23 $\begin{array}{r}3\\ \times 8\\ \hline \end{array}$	24 $\begin{array}{r}5\\ \times 8\\ \hline \end{array}$
25 $\begin{array}{r}5\\ \times 5\\ \hline \end{array}$	26 $\begin{array}{r}7\\ \times 9\\ \hline \end{array}$	27 $\begin{array}{r}7\\ \times 3\\ \hline \end{array}$	28 $\begin{array}{r}6\\ \times 6\\ \hline \end{array}$		
29 $\begin{array}{r}9\\ \times 9\\ \hline \end{array}$	30 $\begin{array}{r}4\\ \times 4\\ \hline \end{array}$	31 $\begin{array}{r}8\\ \times 8\\ \hline \end{array}$	32 $\begin{array}{r}4\\ \times 5\\ \hline \end{array}$		
33 $\begin{array}{r}8\\ \times 5\\ \hline \end{array}$	34 $\begin{array}{r}9\\ \times 7\\ \hline \end{array}$	35 $\begin{array}{r}4\\ \times 8\\ \hline \end{array}$	36 $\begin{array}{r}9\\ \times 5\\ \hline \end{array}$		

Division

Copy and complete.

         5

1 3) 15   2 4) 12   3 5) 40   4 2) 12

5 5) 10   6 6) 6   7 5) 25   8 3) 9

9 3) 18   10 4) 16   11 7) 56   12 5) 15

13 7) 42   14 3) 21   15 6) 54   16 7) 63

17 4) 20   18 6) 18   19 6) 48   20 7) 35

21 4) 24   22 5) 20   23 5) 45   24 3) 24

25 6) 24   26 7) 49   27 7) 21   28 2) 18

29 4) 32   30 2) 0   31 4) 28   32 2) 16

33 6) 30   34 7) 14   35 3) 27   36 5) 35

37 6) 36   38 4) 36   39 6) 42   40 7) 28

A riddle

Divide. Then decode to answer the riddle.
What is the best way to make a hat last?

1 $18 \div 6 =$ _____

2 $56 \div 7 =$ _____

3 $30 \div 6 =$ _____

4 $42 \div 7 =$ _____

8 $24 \div 6 =$ _____

9 $50 \div 5 =$ _____

5 $28 \div 4 =$ _____

6 $14 \div 7 =$ _____

7 $36 \div 6 =$ _____

10 $48 \div 6 =$ _____

11 $63 \div 7 =$ _____

12 $1 \div 1 =$ _____

13 $7 \div 7 =$ _____

14 $0 \div 6 =$ _____

15 $54 \div 6 =$ _____

16 $16 \div 4 =$ _____

17 $49 \div 7 =$ _____

0	1	2	3	4	5	6	7	8	9	10
I	F	H	M	S	K	E	T	A	R	C

Cross-number puzzle. Multiplication

Copy the cross-number square.

First solve all the **across** clues. Then solve any **down** clues that you need to complete the puzzle.

Check your work by solving the rest of the **down** clues.

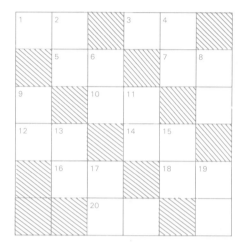

Across		Down	
1	6 × 8	2	9 × 9
3	9 × 9	4	4 × 4
5	3 × 5	6	6 × 9
7	7 × 9	8	6 × 6
10	9 × 5	9	9 × 3
12	8 × 9	11	7 × 8
14	8 × 8	13	3 × 7
16	3 × 4	15	6 × 7
18	5 × 5	17	8 × 3
20	4 × 10	19	10 × 5

More multiplication

Work out the number in the brackets first.

$4 \times (2 + 5) = 28$

7

Copy and complete.

1   $3 \times (2 \times 4) =$ _____

2   $(3 \times 2) \times 4 =$ _____

3   $(3 + 2) \times 4 =$ _____

4   $(5 + 3) + 2 =$ _____

5   $5 + (3 + 2) =$ _____

6   $5 \times (3 + 2) =$ _____

7   $(12 - 4) + 2 =$ _____

8   $12 - (4 + 2) =$ _____

9   $12 - (4 - 2) =$ _____

10   $6 \times (4 \times 0) =$ _____

11   $9 \times (3 \times 2) =$ _____

12   $9 \times (3 + 2) =$ _____

13   $(5 + 2) \times 6 =$ _____

14   $(7 + 2) \times 7 =$ _____

15   $(3 + 5) \times 9 =$ _____

16   $(9 - 4) \times 6 =$ _____

17   $(10 - 3) \times 2 =$ _____

18   $(8 - 2) \times 8 =$ _____

19   $(7 \times 3) + 4 =$ _____

20   $(9 \times 5) + 3 =$ _____

21   $(8 \times 2) + 9 =$ _____

22   $(6 \times 5) - 8 =$ _____

23   $(4 \times 2) - 1 =$ _____

24   $(5 \times 7) - 2 =$ _____

25   $9 \times (4 - 2) =$ _____

26   $8 \times (7 - 4) =$ _____

27   $7 \times (6 - 2) =$ _____

28   $8 \times (5 + 3) =$ _____

29   $6 \times (2 + 7) =$ _____

30   $5 \times (8 + 1) =$ _____

$3 +$ 2×4

Circus report

8 cars took our class to the circus. There was an adult to drive and 3 children in each car. Children paid £2 each to go in and adults paid £3 each.

There were 5 clowns, 6 acrobats, 4 jugglers, 3 dancers, 2 magicians and 9 other people performing.

1 (a) How many people went to the circus altogether?
  (b) How many of them were children?

2 How much was paid (a) by the children?
                    (b) by the adults?
                    (c) altogether?

3 What was the total number of people doing acts at the circus?

4 The clowns performed for 22 minutes, the acrobats for 15 minutes, the jugglers for 17 minutes. The dancing took 9 minutes and the magicians did tricks for 19 minutes. The other acts took a total of 37 minutes.
  (a) How long was the whole performance?
  (b) How much longer did the clowns perform than the magicians?

Finding answers

1 Each child has 8 marbles
   (a) how many marbles if there are (i)   6 children?
                                     (ii)   9 children?
                                    (iii) 10 children?
   (b) Tom, Jenny and Karl each have 8 marbles.
       Tom wins 5 marbles from Jenny.
       Tom then loses 3 marbles to Karl.
       How many marbles do they have each?

2 A marble costs 9p.
   (a) What is the cost of (i)   4 marbles?
                          (ii)   7 marbles?
                         (iii) 10 marbles?
   (b) How many marbles could you buy with
       (i) 81p?   (ii) 54p?   (iii) 45p?

3 Dan had 20 marbles, Chris had 27 marbles and Sue had 31 marbles.
   (a) How many marbles have they got altogether?
   (b) How many more marbles has Sue got than (i) Dan?   (ii) Chris?
   (c) Chris won half of Dan's marbles, but lost 17 marbles to Sue.
       How many marbles did they have each?

Missing factors

Find each missing factor.

__8__ × 5 = 40

1   4 × ____ = 24

2   ____ × 7 = 49

3   3 × ____ = 15

4   7 × ____ = 7

5   ____ × 9 = 45

6   9 × ____ = 72

7   3 × ____ = 27

8   ____ × 8 = 0

9   6 × ____ = 48

10   ____ × 6 = 54

11   6 × ____ = 42

12   5 × ____ = 35

13   ____ × 3 = 3

14   ____ × 6 = 0

15   2 × ____ = 18

16   ____ × 4 = 28

17   8 × ____ = 40

18   ____ × 1 = 9

19   ____ × 8 = 32

20   ____ × 9 = 54

21   8 × ____ = 56

22   ____ × 8 = 72

23   2 × ____ = 16

24   6 × ____ = 36

25   ____ × 3 = 24

26   7 × ____ = 63

27   ____ × 9 = 81

28   6 × ____ = 18

29   4 × ____ = 16

30   ____ × 2 = 14

31   5 × ____ = 30

32   9 × ____ = 27

33   5 × ____ = 25

34   ____ × 4 = 20

35   9 × ____ = 36

36   7 × ____ = 21

37   ____ × 7 = 56

38   ____ × 7 = 42

39   5 × ____ = 20

Selling raffle tickets

Class 5C are selling raffle tickets in aid of 'Save the Children'. Each book contains 10 tickets. Each ticket cost 9p.

1 What is the cost of
   (a) 7 tickets? (b) 4 tickets? (c) 8 tickets? (d) 6 tickets?

2 (a) How much will 1 book of tickets cost?
   (b) How much would you pay for
      (i) 2 books of tickets? (ii) 3 books of tickets? (iii) 1 book and 4 tickets?

3 How many tickets could you buy with
   (a) 54p? (b) 27p? (c) 45p? (d) 81p?

4 You have £5. How much would you have left if you buy
   (a) 9 tickets? (b) 1 book and 7 tickets? (c) 2 books and 4 tickets?

5 Use a calculator to find the answers to these questions.
   (a) The class sold 413 tickets.
       How much money did they collect?
   (b) Class 5B collected £47.07
      (i) What is this in pence?
      (ii) How many tickets did they sell?
   (c) How much would be collected if 19 books and 8 tickets were sold?

Graphs

Sales of Ice Cream

| Sunday | Monday | Tuesday | Wednesday | Thursday | Friday | Saturday |

Each  stands for 10 ice creams sold.

1 What do you think  stands for?

2 What do these stand for?

(a) (b)

3 Draw pictures to show:
  (a) 20 ice creams; (b) 50 ice creams; (c) 35 ice creams.

4 (a) On which day were most ice creams sold?
  (b) How many were sold that day?

5 What was the total number of ice creams sold:
  (a) on Sunday and Thursday?
  (b) in the whole week?

Find the answer

Copy.

Follow the path to find the missing numbers.

1

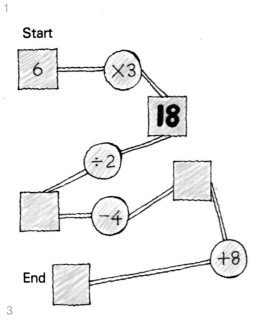

2

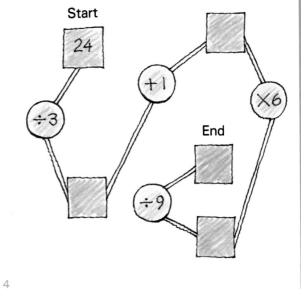

3

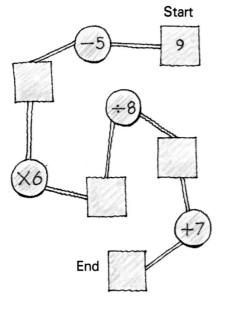

4

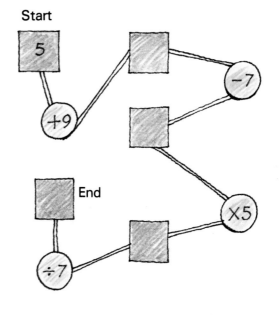

Find the answer

Copy.
Follow the path to find the missing numbers.

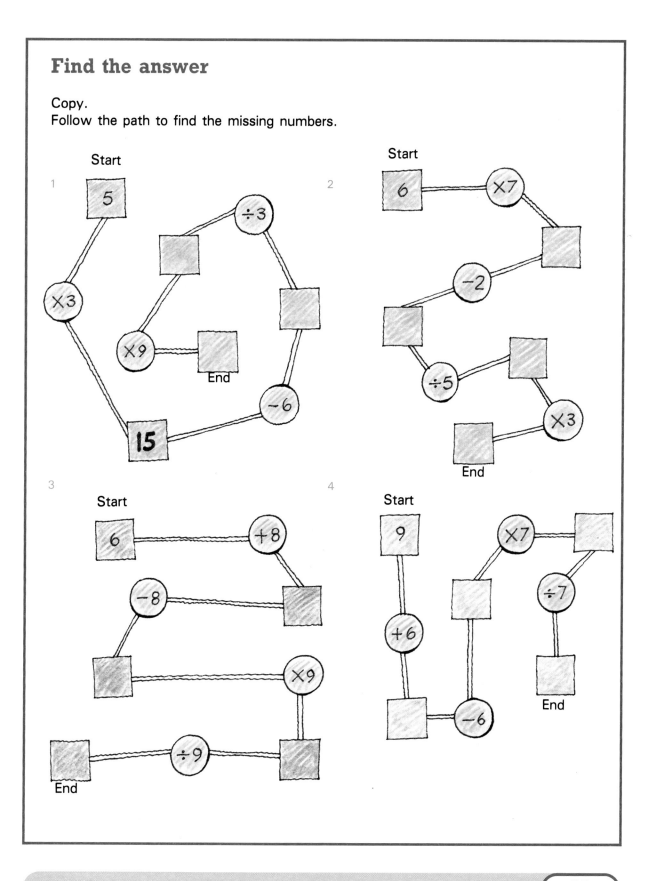

Fractions

3 parts are shaded
5 equal parts

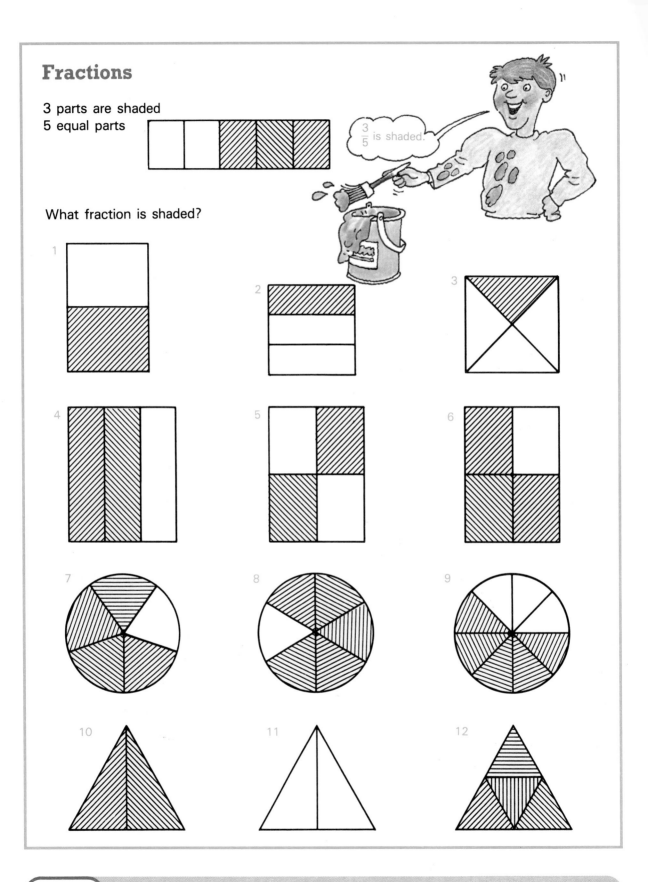

$\frac{3}{5}$ is shaded.

What fraction is shaded?

1

2

3

4

5

6

7

8

9

10

11

12

More fractions

Find the fraction that is:

1 tigers? $\frac{2}{6}$

2 elephants? ____

3 seals? ____

4 **not** seals? ____

5 **not** tigers? ____

6 **not** elephants? ____

7 lions? ____

8 monkeys? ____

9 giraffes? ____

10 **not** giraffes? ____

11 **not** monkeys? ____

12 **not** lions? ____

13 apes? ____

14 zebras? ____

15 camels? ____

16 **not** camels? ____

17 **not** zebras? ____

18 **not** apes? ____

Equations

To find $\frac{1}{4}$ of a number, divide that number by 4.

$\frac{1}{4}$ of $8 = 2$

Copy and complete.

1 $\frac{1}{2}$ of $20 =$ _____   2 $\frac{1}{2}$ of $24 =$ _____   3 $\frac{1}{3}$ of $15 =$ _____   4 $\frac{1}{4}$ of $16 =$ _____

5 $\frac{1}{5}$ of $10 =$ _____   6 $\frac{1}{3}$ of $18 =$ _____   7 $\frac{1}{2}$ of $14 =$ _____   8 $\frac{1}{4}$ of $24 =$ _____

9 $\frac{1}{3}$ of $27 =$ _____   10 $\frac{1}{2}$ of $22 =$ _____   11 $\frac{1}{4}$ of $40 =$ _____   12 $\frac{1}{6}$ of $12 =$ _____

13 $\frac{1}{5}$ of $15 =$ _____   14 $\frac{1}{3}$ of $36 =$ _____   15 $\frac{1}{2}$ of $18 =$ _____   16 $\frac{1}{4}$ of $48 =$ _____

17 $\frac{1}{5}$ of $45 =$ _____   18 $\frac{1}{6}$ of $30 =$ _____   19 $\frac{1}{3}$ of $33 =$ _____   20 $\frac{1}{2}$ of $16 =$ _____

21 $\frac{1}{6}$ of $36 =$ _____   22 $\frac{1}{8}$ of $80 =$ _____   23 $\frac{1}{4}$ of $44 =$ _____   24 $\frac{1}{3}$ of $30 =$ _____

25 $\frac{1}{5}$ of $20 =$ _____   26 $\frac{1}{8}$ of $32 =$ _____   27 $\frac{1}{6}$ of $60 =$ _____   28 $\frac{1}{8}$ of $72 =$ _____

29 $\frac{1}{6}$ of $66 =$ _____   30 $\frac{1}{5}$ of $50 =$ _____   31 $\frac{1}{8}$ of $88 =$ _____   32 $\frac{1}{5}$ of $60 =$ _____

33 $\frac{1}{8}$ of $56 =$ _____   34 $\frac{1}{6}$ of $48 =$ _____   35 $\frac{1}{8}$ of $40 =$ _____   36 $\frac{1}{5}$ of $35 =$ _____

Instructions

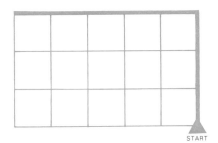

1 (a) Copy and complete so a rectangle
will be drawn.
FORWARD 30 LEFT 90
FORWARD 50 LEFT ...
FORWARD ... .
....

START

Complete this shorter way of drawing the rectangle above.
REPEAT 2 [FORWARD 30 LEFT 90
....]

2 Write the instructions to draw a rectangle 2 units by 4 units.

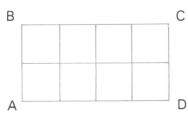

B   C

A   D

(a) Start at A   (b) Start at B

(c) Start at C   (d) Start at D

3 Write the instructions for drawing this rectangle.

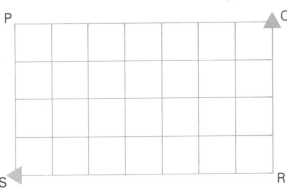

P   Q

S   R

(a) using the word BACK and
starting at S and facing left. (Look
carefully at the picture to see
which way the Turtle is facing).
(b) using the words FORWARD, BACK
and LEFT, (but not right) starting at Q.
(Look carefully again).

4 Write instructions for drawing a square with sides of 9 units.

Symmetry

Copy or trace the shapes.
Draw all the lines of symmetry.

STAGE 28   Lines of symmetry

Multiplying a 2-digit number

Step 1.
Multiply units.

Step 2.
Multiply tens.

```
    23
  ×  2
  ─────
     6
```

```
    23
  ×  2
  ─────
    46
```

Multiply.

1 11 × 7	2 14 × 2	3 23 × 1	4 33 × 3	5 30 ×2	6 12 ×4
7 15 × 1	8 13 × 2	9 22 × 4	10 41 × 2	11 32 × 2	12 40 × 2
13 12 × 3	14 11 × 9	15 24 × 2	16 13 × 3	17 21 × 3	18 22 × 3
19 41 × 1	20 21 × 2	21 33 × 2	22 31 × 2	23 42 × 2	24 30 × 3
25 20 × 3	26 31 × 3	27 10 × 7	28 43 × 2	29 34 × 2	30 21 × 4

Solve.

31 2 days.
How many
hours?

32 23 tricycles.
How many
wheels?

33 4 years.
How many
months?

34 11 dogs.
How many
legs?

Multiplication

Step 1.
Multiply units.

Step 2.
Multiply tens.

$$\begin{array}{r} 42 \\ \times\ 4 \\ \hline 8 \end{array}$$

$$\begin{array}{r} 42 \\ \times 4 \\ \hline 168 \end{array}$$

Multiply.

1	2	3	4	5	6
21 ×6	53 ×3	30 ×6	32 ×4	41 ×5	52 ×3

7	8	9	10	11	12
52 ×4	61 ×7	82 ×4	41 ×4	50 ×7	62 ×2

13	14	15	16	17	18
74 ×2	21 ×9	93 ×2	60 ×5	31 ×7	42 ×3

19	20	21	22	23	24
54 ×2	81 ×7	64 ×2	73 ×3	71 ×5	50 ×4

25	26	27	28	29	30
50 ×6	84 ×2	81 ×5	63 ×2	51 ×6	62 ×4

Solve.

31 52 sheep.
How many
legs?

32 21 weeks.
How many
days?

33 30 hands.
How many
fingers?

34 82 cars.
How many
wheels?

Multiplication with regrouping

Step 1.	Step 2.	Step 3.
Multiply units.	Regroup 20 units for 2 tens.	Multiply tens and add the 2 tens from regrouping.

$$\begin{array}{r} 18 \\ \times\ 3 \\ \hline \end{array}$$

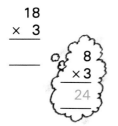

$$\begin{array}{r} 8 \\ \times 3 \\ \hline 24 \end{array}$$

$$\begin{array}{r} 18 \\ \times\ 3 \\ \hline 4 \\ {\scriptstyle 2} \end{array}$$

$$\begin{array}{r} 18 \\ \times\ 3 \\ \hline 54 \\ {\scriptstyle 2} \end{array}$$

Multiply.

1. $\begin{array}{r}38\\ \times\ 4\\ \hline\end{array}$	2. $\begin{array}{r}36\\ \times\ 3\\ \hline\end{array}$	3. $\begin{array}{r}29\\ \times\ 2\\ \hline\end{array}$	4. $\begin{array}{r}39\\ \times\ 6\\ \hline\end{array}$	5. $\begin{array}{r}28\\ \times\ 8\\ \hline\end{array}$	6. $\begin{array}{r}37\\ \times\ 4\\ \hline\end{array}$
7. $\begin{array}{r}67\\ \times\ 7\\ \hline\end{array}$	8. $\begin{array}{r}45\\ \times\ 4\\ \hline\end{array}$	9. $\begin{array}{r}27\\ \times\ 5\\ \hline\end{array}$	10. $\begin{array}{r}49\\ \times\ 5\\ \hline\end{array}$	11. $\begin{array}{r}43\\ \times\ 7\\ \hline\end{array}$	12. $\begin{array}{r}46\\ \times\ 9\\ \hline\end{array}$
13. $\begin{array}{r}95\\ \times\ 7\\ \hline\end{array}$	14. $\begin{array}{r}44\\ \times\ 8\\ \hline\end{array}$	15. $\begin{array}{r}68\\ \times\ 9\\ \hline\end{array}$	16. $\begin{array}{r}47\\ \times\ 9\\ \hline\end{array}$	17. $\begin{array}{r}85\\ \times\ 2\\ \hline\end{array}$	18. $\begin{array}{r}53\\ \times\ 8\\ \hline\end{array}$
19. $\begin{array}{r}48\\ \times\ 8\\ \hline\end{array}$	20. $\begin{array}{r}54\\ \times\ 6\\ \hline\end{array}$	21. $\begin{array}{r}84\\ \times\ 5\\ \hline\end{array}$	22. $\begin{array}{r}93\\ \times\ 7\\ \hline\end{array}$	23. $\begin{array}{r}63\\ \times\ 6\\ \hline\end{array}$	24. $\begin{array}{r}78\\ \times\ 6\\ \hline\end{array}$

Solve.

25. How much for 6?

26. How much for 5 kilograms?

27. Mark delivers 78 papers each day. How many does he deliver in 6 days?

28. Miriam practices her trumpet for 45 minutes each day. How many minutes does she practice for in one week?

Multiplication of money

Multiply. Give your answers (a) in pence; (b) in pounds.

1	64p × 2	2	31p × 5	3	54p × 4	4	29p × 6	5	82p × 8

Multiply. Give your answers in pounds.

6	£76 × 7	7	£16 × 10	8	£33 × 9	9	£47 × 3	10	£68 × 5

11	£0.84 × 2	12	£0.91 × 8	13	£0.63 × 6	14	£0.74 × 5	15	£0.55 × 4

Solve.

16 How much for:
(a) 5 bats?
(b) 7 bats?
(c) 9 bats?

17 How much for:
(a) 4 magazines?
(b) 6 magazines?
(c) 10 magazines?

18 How much for:
(a) 2 packets?
(b) 8 packets?
(c) 9 packets?

19 How much for:
(a) 3 radios?
(b) 5 radios?
(c) 8 radios?

Money multiplication

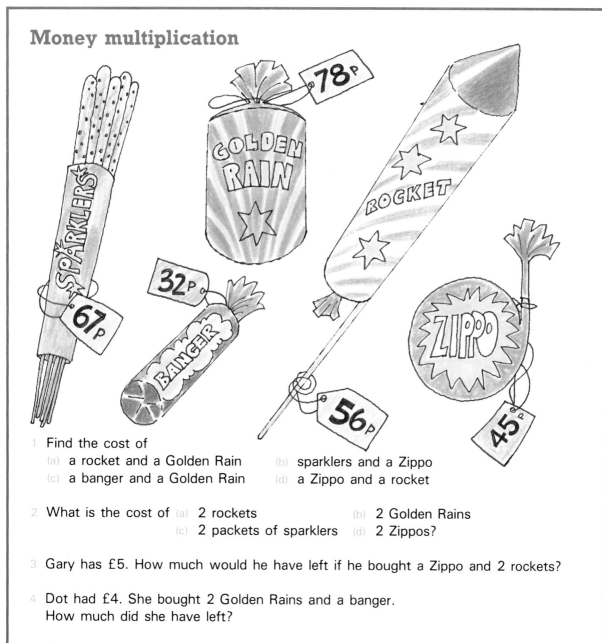

1 Find the cost of
   (a) a rocket and a Golden Rain
   (b) sparklers and a Zippo
   (c) a banger and a Golden Rain
   (d) a Zippo and a rocket

2 What is the cost of (a) 2 rockets
   (b) 2 Golden Rains
   (c) 2 packets of sparklers
   (d) 2 Zippos?

3 Gary has £5. How much would he have left if he bought a Zippo and 2 rockets?

4 Dot had £4. She bought 2 Golden Rains and a banger.
   How much did she have left?

5 Find the total cost of these:
   (a) 3 rockets at 56p each
   2 Zippos at 45p each
   1 Golden Rain at 78p
   4 bangers at 32p each

   (b) 2 packets of sparklers at 67p each
   3 Golden Rains at 78p each
   2 bangers at 32p each
   5 rockets at 56p each.

6 Find the prices of any things you like from a shop or catalogue. (For example they could be sweets, or toys, or fireworks). Make up bills like these in Question 5 and find the totals.

Dividing a 2-digit number

Step 1.
Divide tens.

$$\begin{array}{r} 3 \\ 3\overline{)\,96} \end{array}$$

Step 2.
Divide units.

$$\begin{array}{r} 32 \\ 3\overline{)\,96} \end{array}$$

Divide.

1 $2\overline{)\,28}$ 2 $3\overline{)\,33}$ 3 $2\overline{)\,40}$ 4 $3\overline{)\,30}$ 5 $2\overline{)\,46}$

6 $2\overline{)\,68}$ 7 $3\overline{)\,69}$ 8 $3\overline{)\,36}$ 9 $2\overline{)\,86}$ 10 $3\overline{)\,90}$

11 $2\overline{)\,60}$ 12 $6\overline{)\,60}$ 13 $2\overline{)\,84}$ 14 $4\overline{)\,48}$ 15 $3\overline{)\,63}$

16 $4\overline{)\,88}$ 17 $2\overline{)\,48}$ 18 $3\overline{)\,93}$ 19 $7\overline{)\,70}$ 20 $2\overline{)\,88}$

21 $3\overline{)\,66}$ 22 $9\overline{)\,99}$ 23 $4\overline{)\,40}$ 24 $3\overline{)\,39}$ 25 $5\overline{)\,50}$

26 $8\overline{)\,88}$ 27 $3\overline{)\,60}$ 28 $2\overline{)\,64}$ 29 $4\overline{)\,84}$ 30 $7\overline{)\,77}$

31 $3\overline{)\,99}$ 32 $8\overline{)\,80}$ 33 $5\overline{)\,55}$ 34 $9\overline{)\,90}$ 35 $6\overline{)\,66}$

STAGE 33   Division by single digit practice: no remainders

Division with regrouping

Step 1.	Step 2.	Step 3.
Divide tens. and subtract.	Regroup the 2 units and the 1 ten which is left.	Divide units. and subtract.

Step 1.
```
      1
   4) 52
   − 4    tens
      1    ten left
```

Step 2.
```
      1
   4) 52
   −40    (same as 4 tens)
     12
```

Step 3.
```
     13
   4) 52
   −40
     12
   −12
      0
```

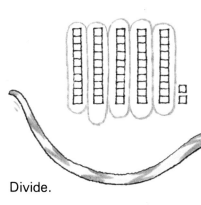

Divide.

1 $3\overline{)75}$	2 $2\overline{)38}$	3 $3\overline{)81}$	4 $4\overline{)56}$	5 $2\overline{)56}$
6 $6\overline{)96}$	7 $3\overline{)78}$	8 $2\overline{)76}$	9 $5\overline{)75}$	10 $3\overline{)72}$
11 $3\overline{)57}$	12 $2\overline{)58}$	13 $4\overline{)64}$	14 $3\overline{)45}$	15 $6\overline{)84}$
16 $5\overline{)95}$	17 $2\overline{)94}$	18 $6\overline{)72}$	19 $2\overline{)78}$	20 $4\overline{)72}$
21 $4\overline{)96}$	22 $5\overline{)85}$	23 $7\overline{)98}$	24 $5\overline{)65}$	25 $2\overline{)98}$

Solve.

26 91 days.
How many weeks?

27 84 sides.
How many triangles?

28 80 toes.
How many feet?

29 62 wheels.
How many bicycles?

Division with remainder

Step 1.
Divide tens.
and subtract.

Step 2.
Regroup.

Step 3.
Divide units
and subtract.

Step 4.
Write the
remainder.

```
      1
  4) 79
  − 4    tens
    3    tens left
```

```
      1
  4) 79
  − 40
    39
```

```
     19
  4) 79
  − 40
    39
  − 36
     3
```

```
     19 R3
  4) 79
  − 40
    39
  − 36
     3
```

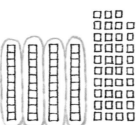

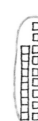
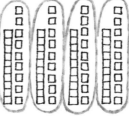

Divide.

1 2) 83	2 3) 68	3 6) 86	4 2) 67	5 5) 78
6 8) 91	7 4) 59	8 2) 75	9 4) 50	10 6) 62
11 7) 94	12 5) 88	13 6) 93	14 2) 85	15 4) 83
16 4) 55	17 2) 79	18 5) 77	19 9) 93	20 7) 87
21 7) 73	22 5) 63	23 3) 76	24 7) 92	25 4) 81
26 5) 92	27 4) 62	28 7) 88	29 6) 87	30 8) 95
31 8) 83	32 5) 76	33 3) 92	34 4) 71	35 7) 85

Division of money

Divide. Use your calculator when you want to.

1 2) 86p   2 3) 93p   3 4) 80p

4 3) £69   5 5) £95   6 2) £61.00

7 6) £75.00   8 4) £92.00   9 10) £76.00

10 Samir bought some sweets costing 2p each.
    (a) How many sweets could he buy with 43p?
    (b) How much would he have left?

11 Three girls share £19.50 equally.
    How much will they each get?

12 Harry had £22. He bought some rose bushes costing £3 each.
    (a) How many rose bushes could he buy?
    (b) How much money would he have left?

13 A school had £47.30 to spend on books costing £6 each.
    (a) How many books could they buy?
    (b) How much money would be left?

14 Another school had £52.40 to spend on books.
    They bought 9 books. The books all cost the same amount.
    They had £2 left over.
    How much did each book cost?

Measuring

Measure the length of each line.
Then find the perimeter of each shape.

STAGE 36   Measuring length: cm

Area

Give each area in square centimetres.

10 Copy this table. Complete it by working out the area of each rectangle.

length (cm)	2	6	7	4	5	7	9	8	8
width (cm)	7	6	8	9	8	9	6	8	9
area (square cm)									

Remember that the area of a rectangle = length × width

Area and perimeter

Give each area and perimeter.

1

2

3

4

5 Use centimetre-squared paper. Draw shapes with:
  (a) area 6 cm², perimeter 14 cm.
  (b) area 15 cm², perimeter 16 cm.
  (c) area 13 cm², perimeter 16 cm.
  (d) area 8 cm², perimeter 14 cm.

STAGE 37 Area (cm²) and perimeter (cm)

Volume

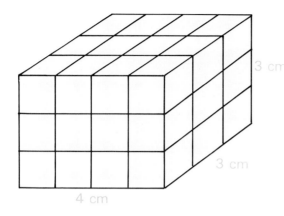

Remember that
volume = length × width × height.

The volume of this box is
4 cm × 3 cm × 3 cm = 36 cubic cm

Give each volume in cubic centimetres.

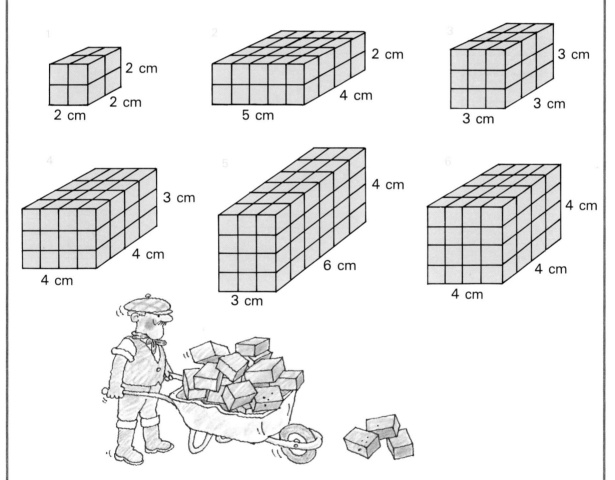

The sum of the volumes above should be 259 cubic centimetres.

Volume

Copy and complete this table using the shapes below.

	Length in cm	Width in cm	Height in cm	Volume in cubic cm
1				
2				
3				
4				
5				
6				
7				
8				
9				

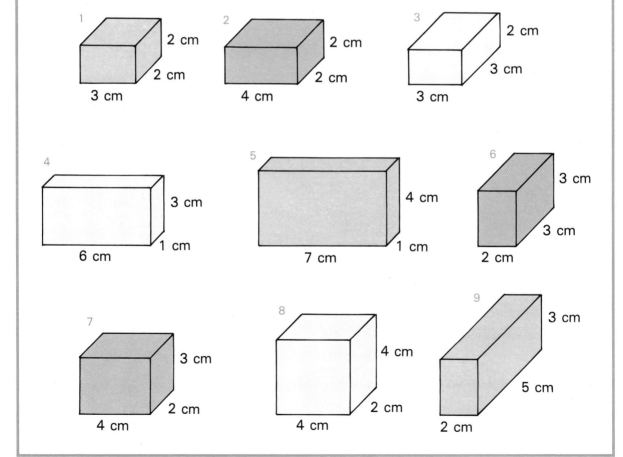

Collecting tallies

Joe and Azza made a tally chart to show which day of the week the pupils in their year liked best. This is what their tally chart looked like:

Remember ⏚ stands for 5.

1 Copy and complete the tally chart.

	Tallies	Frequency
Sunday	ⅢⅢ ⅢⅢ ⅢⅢ |||	18
Monday	ⅢⅢ ⅢⅢ	
Tuesday	ⅢⅢ ⅢⅢ ||	
Wednesday	ⅢⅢ ||||	
Thursday	ⅢⅢ ⅢⅢ		
Friday	ⅢⅢ ⅢⅢ ⅢⅢ	
Saturday	ⅢⅢ ⅢⅢ ⅢⅢ ⅢⅢ ||	

Fill in the 'Frequency' column.
What is the total of the frequencies?

2 (a) Make a tally chart for the pupils in your class, showing which day of the week they like best.
(b) Use squared paper and draw a block graph to show the result from (a)

3

Colours	Tallies	Frequency
Blue		
Black		
Red		
Yellow		
White		
Silver		

Make a list of six colours for cars. (Choose your own colours)
Ask everyone in your class which of the six colours they would choose for a car.

Record the tallies and find the frequency for each colour.
Add the frequencies.
Draw a block graph to represent your results.

Problem solving

The numbers have been replaced by  ⬤ and ▢
You have to decide whether to **add**, **subtract**, **multiply** or **divide**.

column
← row

1 Su-Lin did ⬤ equations every minute.
   How many did she do in ▢ minutes?

2 There are ▢ stamps
   on each sheet
   and ⬤ stamps in each column.
   How many stamps are there in each
   row?

3 A woman earned £ ▢ one week and
   £⬤ the next week.
   How much did she earn altogether?

4 Sally's heart beats ⬤ times each
   minute.
   How many times will it beat in ▢
   minutes?

5 A grocer had ▢ kilograms of flour.
   He sold ⬤ kilograms.
   How many kilograms of flour did he
   have left?

6 The distance from Glasgow to London
   is ⬤ kilometres. How much further
   have I to go, if I have travelled ▢
   kilometres of the journey?

7 John weighed ▢ kilograms. He went
   on a diet and lost ⬤ kilograms.
   How much did he then weigh?

8 There were ▢ boys and ⬤ girls at a
   party.
   How many children were there at the
   party?

9 ⬤ tickets for a disco cost a total of
   £ ▢ .
   What is the cost of each ticket?

10 A television programme started at ▢
   minutes to 8 and lasted for ⬤
   minutes. At what time did the
   programme finish?

Number patterns with nines

This is a column ↓

1	2	3	4	5	6	7	8	9
10	11	12	13	14	15	16	17	18
19	20	21	22	23	24	25	26	27
28	29	30	31	32	33	34	35	36
37	38	39	40	41	42	43	44	45
46	47	48	49	50	51	52	53	54
55	56	57	58	59	60	61	62	63
64	65	66	67	68	69	70	71	72
73	74	75	76	77	78	79	80	81

← This is a row

1 4, 13, 22, 31, 40.

(a) Find these numbers on the '81 square'.
What are the next three numbers?

(b) Subtract each number from the following one.
For example: 13 − 4
What do you notice about your answers?

(c) Without looking at the '81 square', can you write down all the numbers in the column with the top number 6?

2 Start with 2. Look at the numbers in the diagonal like this:

2
12

(a) Write down all the numbers in that diagonal, finishing with 72.
(b) What is the difference between each number and the following one?
(c) Start with any other number in the top row. You should find that the numbers on the diagonal always increase by 10. This is true for every set of diagonal numbers.
Why?

3 Look at 7 and the numbers on this diagonal:
(a) Write down all the numbers on this diagonal finishing at 55.
(b) Start at any other number you like on the '81 square'.
Write down the numbers on that diagonal.
What do you notice about the difference between each number and the following one?

7
15

Roman numbers

I	V	X	L	C	D	M
1	5	10	50	100	500	1000

Remember If a symbol for a smaller number is written to the left of the symbol for a larger number, then subtract.

Example IX = 9 (10 − 1)   LM = 950 (1000 − 50)

1 Write in our number system
   (a) III (b) IV (c) XXI (d) CL (e) MDX
   (f) DLV (g) CIX (h) LIV (i) XXVIII (j) MMIC

2 Write in Roman numbers
   (a) 8 (b) 11 (c) 19 (d) 27 (e) 41 (f) 54
   (g) 106 (h) 402 (i) 990 (j) 1060 (k) 2099

3 Write the present year in Roman numbers.

4 Find out the year when these events happened, then write them as Roman numbers
   (a) The Battle of Hastings.
   (b) Guy Fawkes tried to blow up Parliament.
   (c) The Spanish Armada was destroyed.
   (d) The year in which you were born.
   (e) The year in which you will be 100 years old.

Multiplying by ten

To find the total number of pencils, you can multiply.

$$\begin{array}{r} 5 \\ \times\ 10 \\ \hline 50 \end{array}$$

I write the 0 first and then multiply 5 by 1.

Multiply.

1. 14 × 10 ———	2. 16 × 10 ———	3. 18 × 10 ———	4. 23 × 10 ———	5. 27 × 10 ———
6. 39 × 10 ———	7. 54 × 10 ———	8. 67 × 10 ———	9. 73 × 10 ———	10. 95 × 10 ———
11. 127 × 10 ———	12. 158 × 10 ———	13. 146 × 10 ———	14. 185 × 10 ———	15. 170 × 10 ———
16. 220 × 10 ———	17. 243 × 10 ———	18. 327 × 10 ———	19. 468 × 10 ———	20. 562 × 10 ———
21. 671 × 10 ———	22. 700 × 10 ———	23. 754 × 10 ———	24. 833 × 10 ———	25. 976 × 10 ———

Solve.

26 24 pairs of hands.
How many fingers?

27 42 ten pence pieces.
How many pennies?

28 Alan put 10 stamps on each page of his stamp album.
How many stamps can he put on 58 pages?

29 Each week Mrs Johnson's class learns 10 new words.
How many words do they learn in 26 weeks?

Problem solving

Solve. (Use your calculator if you like).

1 The school library has 846 fiction books and 687 books that are not fiction.
  (a) How many books are there altogether?
  (b) How many more books are fiction than are not fiction?

2 A shelf holds 80 books.
  How many books on:
  (a) 2 shelves? (b) 5 shelves? (c) 7 shelves? (d) 10 shelves?

3 One day there were 916 books in the library.
  416 were then taken out and 297 were returned.
  How many books were there in the library?

4 94 new books were bought. Six children helped to put plastic covers on them.
  Each child covered the same number of books and only the left over books were
  done by the teacher
  (a) How many covers did each child fit?
  (b) How many books remained for the teacher to cover?

5 Plastic covers cost 26p each, but are only sold in packets of 10.
  (a) What is the cost of one packet of covers?
  (b) How many packets must have been bought to cover the 94 new books?
  (c) What was the total cost of the covers for the new books?

Tenths

How many squares are coloured?
Give your answer in figures and in words.

1.6   one point six

STAGE 51   Decimals

55

Decimals

1

8.0　　8.1　　8.2　　　　　　　　　　　　　　　　　　　8.9　　9.0

(a) Copy and complete the number line
(b) Mark your number like this:
　　(i) write A at 8.4.　(ii) Write B at 8.7
(c) Is A nearer to 8.0 or to 9.0?
(d) Is B nearer to 8.0 or to 9.0?

2

A　　　　　　　　B　　　　　　　C　　　　　D
↓　　　　　　　　↓　　　　　　　↓　　　　　↓

18.0　　　　　　　　　　　　　　　　　　　　　　　19.0

What is the value at (a) A　(b) B　(c) C　(d) D?
Round the values at A, B, C and D to the nearest whole number.

3 (a) Is 11.6 nearer to 11 or to 12?
　 (b) Is 7.3 nearer to 7 or to 8?
　 (c) Is 99.7 nearer to 99 or to 100?

4 Round to the nearest whole number
　 (a) 14.1　(b) 26.7　(c) 38.3　(d) 69.9　(e) 80.6

5 Copy and complete by writing > or <
　 (a) 8.6 . . . 9.0　　(b) 14.2 . . . 12.9
　 (c) 80.0 . . . 79.8　(d) 101.1 . . . 96.7

6 4.9, 6.0, 5.6
　 (a) Which of these three numbers is (i) greatest?
　　　　　　　　　　　　　　　　　　　　　　(ii) smallest?
　 (b) Write them in order with the greatest first.

Decimals

Add

1	4.7 + 3.2	2	3.6 + 5.4	3	7.3 + 1.8	4	9.6 + 2.1	5	5.8 + 5.7
6	13.6 + 9.5	7	20.7 + 11.7	8	34.9 + 0.3	9	1.4 + 27.8	10	54.1 + 17.9

Copy and complete.
Add across and down.

11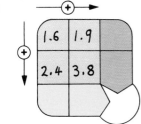

1.6	1.9
2.4	3.8

12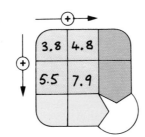

3.8	4.8
5.5	7.9

13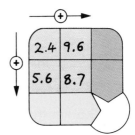

2.4	9.6
5.6	8.7

Subtract

14	4.7 − 2.5	15	6.1 − 4.1	16	5.3 − 2.8	17	6.7 − 4.9	18	9.0 − 2.3
19	11.2 − 4.6	20	14.0 − 9.2	21	25.1 − 16.7	22	31.0 − 14.6	23	44.4 − 27.7

Subtract across and down.
Copy and complete.

24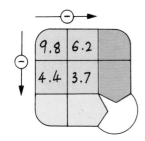

9.8	6.2
4.4	3.7

25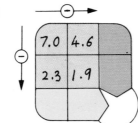

7.0	4.6
2.3	1.9

26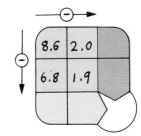

8.6	2.0
6.8	1.9

Number problems with decimals

Solve these number problems.

1   Ahmed weighed 37.8 kg.
    His weight went up by 1.7 kg
    What did he weigh then?

2   A runner took 28.6 seconds to run the first half of a race and 30.1 seconds to run
    the second half.
    (a) What was the total time for the race?
    (b) What was the difference in times for the two halves?

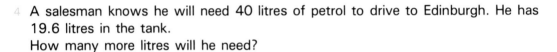

3   An electrician had 17.2 metres of wire.
    She used 9.6 metres.
    How much wire did she then have left?

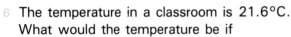

4   A salesman knows he will need 40 litres of petrol to drive to Edinburgh. He has
    19.6 litres in the tank.
    How many more litres will he need?

5   It is 93.5 km from Bigham to Littleton.
    Jill cycles 14.8 km from Bigham to Stopham.
    She has a rest at Stopham, then cycles another 28.9 km towards Littleton.
    (a) How far was Jill from Littleton when she had her rest?
    (b) How far is Jill from Littleton after she has cycled the 28.9 km?

6   The temperature in a classroom is 21.6°C.
    What would the temperature be if
    (a) it rose 1.9°C?
    (b) it dropped 0.8°C?

Decimal problems

1 0.8 metres of string is needed to tie up a parcel.
The string is cut from a length of 3.2 metres.
How much string is left?

2 Phil weighs 31.1 kilograms and Kim weighs 27.6 kilograms.
How much heavier is Phil than Kim?

3 Mr Burton bought 5.2 kilograms of vegetables and 1.9 kilograms of meat.
(a) What was the total weight he bought?
(b) How much heavier were the vegetables than the meat?

4 A lorry driver drove 26.7 kilometres, then had a rest. Then he drove another 49.5
kilometres.
What was the total distance travelled?

5 The temperature one night was 8.9°C.
The next day the temperature rose to 13.2°C.
How much did the temperature rise?

6 Carol ran at 18.4 kilometres per hour and Amy ran at 20.1 kilometres per hour.
Calculate the difference in their speeds.

7 A car had 12.3 litres of petrol in the tank.
It used 3.6 litres and then had 9.5 litres put in its tank.
(a) How much petrol was left in the tank after using the 3.6 litres?
(b) How much petrol was in the tank after the 9.5 litres were put in?

Temperature

1 The picture shows part of the scale of a thermometer.

What is the temperature at (a) A? (b) B? (c) C?

2 Write the temperature at (a) E, (b) F and (c) G

3 What is the difference between these temperatures?
   (a) 14.6°C and 20.1°C   (b) 100°C and 94.5°C
   (c) 2.5°C and − 1.4°C   (d) − 1.8°C and − 2.8°C

4 The temperature in a classroom was 21.4°C.
   (a) What would the temperature be if it rose
        (i) 1.8°C?   (ii) 2.9°C?   (iii) 4.7°C?
   (b) What would the temperature be if it dropped
        (i) 1.5°C?   (ii) 2.6°C?   (iii) 3.8°C?

5 In Moscow one winter day the temperature was − 2.1°C.
   What would the temperature be if it
   (a) rose 3.4°C?   (b) rose 1.9°C?   (c) dropped 0.8°C?   (d) dropped 1.6°C?

6 In Cairo the temperature was 100.8°C.
   It dropped 8.9°C that night but then rose 5.4°C the next day. What was the
   temperature
   (a) after it dropped 8.9°C?   (b) after the rise of 5.4°C?

Probability

No chance   Poor chance   Even chance   Good chance   Certain

For each question your answer is to be one of these terms above.

1   One day I will be a famous artist.

2   At 10 o'clock this evening it will be raining.

3   I will be in to school tomorrow.

4   I will eat an apple in the next 24 hours.

5   One day I will learn to drive a car.

6   I will go to sleep within the next 12 hours.

7   If I toss three coins at least one of them will be a 'head'.

8   You have two dice marked 1 to 6.
    You throw the two dice:-
    (a)   The total shown will be three or more.
    (b)   The difference between the two numbers shown will be 1 or more.
    (c)   The two numbers will be the same.

9   There are 10 white socks and 10 black socks in a drawer.
    You pick 3 socks without looking at them.
    What is the chance you will have two socks the same colour?

Estimation

You have to choose one of the four answers A, B, C or D.

Example
How many lines are there
inside this rectangle?

A 12   B 31   C 46   D more than 100

The correct answer is B.

1   How many lines are there in
    this rectangle?
    A 28   B 82   C 50   D 73

2   How many postage stamps of this size are needed to cover this page?
    A 100   B 56   C 34   D 80

3   How many seconds are there in one week?
    A 604 800   B 3600   C 4 000 000   D 15 640

4   An egg weighs 60 grams.
    A 9 year old boy weighs 42 kilograms.
    Estimate how many eggs are needed to balance the boy's weight.
    A 150   B 4000   C 2680   D 700